What Is Nationalism and What Do Nationalists Want?

Alfredo Rocco

Translated by Richard Robinson

Sunny Lou Publishing Company
Portland, Oregon, USA
http://www.sunnyloupublishing.com

Original Publication Date: October 13, 2025

ISBN: 978-1-955392-82-2

This translation from Italian is based on the Piccola Biblioteca di Propaganda Nazionale dell'Università di Padova edition of *Che cosa è il nazionalismo e cosa vogliono i nazionalisti*, Padua, 1914.

Contents

Introduction

What Is Nationalism and What Do Nationalists Want? by Alfredo Rocco, is the latest in our series of early 20th century works on Italian politics.

Alfredo Rocco (AD 1875 – 1935) was an Italian jurist and politician. Born in Naples, he was the son of engineer Alberto Rocco and Maria Berlingieri. His three other brothers were, like him, all jurists.

He was responsible for, and his name is associated with, the Italian Penal Code (referred to as the *Codice Rocco*) much of which remains in force in Italy today and which he had a direct hand in.

He was Professor of Civil Procedure at the University of Parma from 1906-1909, and at the University of Palermo from 1909-1910. He later taught Economic Legislation of Labor and Commercial Law at the Sapienza University of Rome, where he also served as rector from 1932-1935.

Originally a member of the Italian Radical Party, he become a Nationalist in 1913, while teaching at the University of Padua; it is during this time that he wrote the present work, published in 1914. He was a staunch advocate of Italy's intervention in the First World War (the "the Great War").

From 1920-1922 he was President and Managing Director of *L'Idea Nazionale*, the newspaper co-founded by Enrico Corradini, and the official organ of the Italian Nationalist Association, which later merged with the National Fascist Party in 1923.

Under Mussolini's government, Rocco served as Undersecretary of State, first for the Ministry of the Treasury, then Finance, from 1922 to 1924; in 1924 he was elected President of the Chamber of Deputies. From 1925 to 1932 he was Minister of Justice. From 1934 until his death, he was a Senator of the Kingdom of Italy.

– Richard Robinson, Stumptown, October 12, 2025, on the Anniversary of Christopher Columbus' Landing in the Americas.

What Is Nationalism

What Is Nationalism

For three years now a gust of new life has blown into the closed environment of Italian politics: a breath of youth, faith, and hope. This gust of new life is called **nationalism**. For forty years the Italian political parties had been occupied and preoccupied with the most varied problems: freedom, which nobody threatens anymore; democracy, which is the participation of the people in Government, which, with universal suffrage, has reached the extreme limits of its realization; socialism, or rather, the distribution of that miserable amount of wealth that nature, stingy and stepmotherly toward the Italian people, has allowed us to attain; religion, which is a great and respectable thing, but concerns the inner conscience more than political action; feminism, temperance, and vivisection; but nobody (save Francesco Crispi, who died of a broken heart because of it) had ever spoken to the people about that small and miserable thing called the *Italian nation*. We had forgotten about this one detail: that beyond the individual, beyond the class, beyond humanity, exists the nation, the Italian *race*; and that the individual does not live only in the class, does not live at all in a society of all men, but lives instead and principally in that social aggregate composed of men of his same race, which is the *nation*. It was forgotten that, while humanity today is not an organized social aggregate, and never will be, because societies are formed to safeguard certain common interests, in contrast with the interests of other aggregates, and until we have found ourselves in conflict with inhabitants of the Moon or Mars, humanity as such will not have specific interests to defend, and will therefore not be a true organized society; whereas the multiple classes into which a national society is divided work out their differences within a superior organization or frame-work, the nation, which can and must settle them with justice, a *national* society is the only social aggregate that has serious specific interests to assert, vigorously and constantly challenged by other national societies, and must assert them, necessarily, by itself, with its own forces because no other organization exists supe-rior to the nation that can render justice to the nation.

To occupy and preoccupy ourselves with the incessant struggle that the Italian nation must wage in the world, with its own forces, in order to safeguard the interests of the Italian race, is to practice nationalism.

But is it necessary to practice nationalism? Is it necessary to occupy ourselves with this struggle?

It is necessary.

It is important to remember two points of fact that are too often ignored by Italians.

First. Italian territory is a limited territory, and *naturally poor*. We have too much mountain and too little plain; except for the Po Valley, we have no im-portant rivers; in the Mezzogiorno and on the islands we have no water; our land is exhausted by millennia of agricultural labor, and, to make it produce like the lands of other countries requires major effort and ma-jor expense (consequently, our agriculture cannot compete with that of other countries); we have no iron, and we have no coal; we lack, in short, the necessary raw material for modern heavy industry (consequently our industries cannot compete with foreign industries). Despite all that, sweating and working like no other people has ever done, because none has ever found itself in such dire conditions, we have made marvelous progress. Marvelous, I say, not in an absolute way, because we still remain far, but very far, behind nations favored by nature, like France, England, and Germany (the wealth of Italy is about 80 billion, while that of France is 300, that of England 350, and that of Germany 400); marvelous in view of the difficulties that we have overcome, and the effort that we have made. But even this effort will have a limit. Something remains to be done, especially in the Mezzogiorno, and can be done. But one must not believe that it is very much. The famous *uncultivated lands* to be cultivated, which the Socialists and the ignorant speak of, **do not exist**. *Italy has less uncultivated land than France and England*. And the land that is still uncultivated (with few exceptions) cannot but remain uncultivated, because it is not arable: they are the high and rocky mountains: rivers, torrents, lakes. These sorts of land exist everywhere, and naturally also in Italy. If, by making an extraordinary effort, which may very well be impossible, we were to succeed in *doubling* our wealth, and raising it to 150 billion, we would still have, with a like population, not for our own fault, but for that of nature, a wealth equal to half that of France. **It is a condemnation to poverty, or, at least, to mediocrity**.

Second. The Italian race, which lives on this limited and poor territory, is a *numerous* and *fertile* race. The Italians in the world today number about 42 million, 36 [million] in Italy, and about 6 [million] abroad. **The Italian race is therefore, today, more numerous than the French**, who number no more than 40 million people. And we will continue to be more numerous in the future. We grow at a rate of about 400,000 a year: the French population is stagnant: in fact, if the gaps were not filled by immigration, it would be shrinking. **Now, the number [of people] is the true strength of the race**. Numerous and fertile races are doughty and expansive: they advance and conquer. The Italian race also expands, breaks the reins that bind it to the territory of the fatherland, and it advances. This expansion today is called **emigration**. While politickers debated so many useless things, the Italian race resolved the problem on its own, by initiating Italian expansion. But this expansion has assumed, by necessity, the unhappiest form; the unhappiest both morally and economically. It has presented itself as an *exportation of human merchandise in a foreign land*, and it works under infinite duress, under nameless humiliations, with ineffable miseries, amidst actual human hecatombs, and, above all, under a despicable exploitation. Our workers, these six million Italians who are abroad, save a few fortunate exceptions, live derided, despised by everyone, exploited by their foreign masters.

Well then, who does not see that these two factors – the poverty of the Italian territory; the fertility of the Italian race – put before us a formidable problem, the greatest and most urgent problem of Italian life?

This problem is, first of all, a problem of **justice**.

We ask for justice, finally, also for the Italian nation. We are poor, not because we have not worked, but because our territory is poor. Other nations are rich, not because they have worked more than us, but because either, like France, they possess a rich territory or with violence, like England, they have made themselves masters of others' rich territories. We have had, until now, to endure the injustice of nature, because we were few and the others were many, we were divided and the others were united. Now, we too are united, we too have become many, and we have reached and we have surpassed the others. Now, we too demand our place in the sun. We demand it because it is right that it be given to us too, after so many sufferings and so many miseries. We demand it because, at last, we have the *strength* to demand it.

This problem, then, is a problem of **economic advancement**.

A given: that, through enormous labor, in these last twenty years especially, the Italian nation has made great economic progress, and that it will be able to make even greater progress, with tenacious effort; a given: that before long a moment will come when the poor Italian soil will have given all that it can give; two consequences follow: 1st) We must continue this effort; domestic production must be intensified and brought to the maximum [level] possible, to properly prepare ourselves for the second phase of our economic evolution, the phase of *expansion abroad*. 2nd) Serenely and steadfastly, we must from now on prepare ourselves for the phase of *expansion* o r *conquest*. Whereas other nations have first *conquered* and then *worked*, we will have first *worked* and then *conquered*. Indeed, however hard the work has been, that much easier will the conquest seem, comparatively. With these two phases alone – *domestic production* and *conquest abroad* – we will be able to resolve our economic problem. And let no one say that by now there is nothing left to be conquered because every territory is occupied. *Free territories have never existed*, nor were the territories that constitute the immense British empire today, or those of the colonial empire of France, ever free. *Strong and progressive nations do not conquer free territories,* but territories occupied by nations in decadence. And of these, and rich beyond measure, there are many today, but many, throughout the world. And we will stop there.

Finally, our national problem is a problem of **moral and social advancement**.

Italy is, socially, as yet a primitive country. Less apparent in Northern Italy, the phenomenon is clearest in Southern Italy. But essentially everywhere, Italian society is a disaggregated society; indeed, if an Italian State exists, a single Italian society is only now barely in the process of formation. An Italian, in the north or in the south, feels his national interests only faintly, and feels his individual interests greatly, and those of his group: at most, especially in the north, he will arrive at a strong feeling for the interests of his communal aggregate. This is why national politics in Italy are conducted (a clear contradiction in terms) on a *communal basis*. Consequently, this disaggregation must disappear. And to make it disappear, to construct Italian society solidly, there is but one means: focus the attention of Italians intensely on the struggles that the Italian nation is fighting and will fight in the world. Just as families bond together in their struggles against difficulties and adversities, so too do societies bond in their struggles for affirmation in the world. It has been seen, in this respect, just how helpful the Tripolitanian War was. And when the sensation is vividly felt by all Italians as the Italian nation struggles, on a daily basis, for the conquest of its well-being and power in the world, every one of us will feel like a soldier in this great army arrayed for battle. And each will then understand the need to work, in his own field, with alacrity and zeal; because whoever remains inert in battle is a coward; and we must not disturb the solidarity of the nation with internal discord, because whoever foments discord on a day of battle is a traitor. In the name of the nation, the *national aggregate* will be cemented, the *consciousness of national interests* will be created, *national discipline* will be established.

It is easy to understand that **this great problem of the Italian nation presents itself as preeminent, all-consuming, and that, faced with it, all other problems must appear secondary and subordinate**.

Nationalism is, therefore, also the **affirmation of the absolute preeminence, for Italians, of the problem of prosperity, power, and the future of the Italian nation**.

Italian Political Parties and Nationalism

Italian Political Parties and Nationalism

This position of nationalism, which takes the Italian national problem as preeminent and absorbing, and all other problems as subordinate and secondary, establishes with great clarity its position toward present-day Italian parties, and it explains why nationalists cannot be mistaken for any of the political groupings that exist in Italy today. Nationalism has a characteristic position all its own in the Italian life today, for *it is the unique disposition that gives absolute importance to the national problem*. Nationalists, therefore, are not moderate liberals, or rather, they are not *essentially* moderate liberals, they are not conservatives, they are not clericalists, they are not democrats, nor radicals, nor republicans; they are not, finally, socialists; although they do not deny the value of the problems that each of these parties put forward (which explains how some of them may get along under certain circumstances), they always remain characteristically nationalists, for they alone ascribe absolute value to the national problem and consider all the other problems as subordinate.

Why Nationalists Are Not Moderate Liberals, Nor Conservatives

Liberalism, which even today forms the nucleus of the doctrine of that party that one is commonly referred to as moderate liberal, represents, from the historical point of view, the reaction of individualism against the excesses of an absolutist or autocratic State. Nearly all European nations, during the XIV, XV, and XVI centuries, by necessity of national formation, [i.e.,] the State, organized under monarchic rule almost everywhere, affirmed its preeminence over its individuals and minor groups. In this affirmation, which was nonetheless necessary for the creation of a solidly constitutive national society, they took things too far, as often happens: the individual was absorbed, squeezed, annihilated, and the State became a monopoly of several closed castes, that is, of the nobility and the clergy. These excesses, which culminated in the XVII and XVIII centuries, produced a natural reaction among oppressed individuals; the bourgeoisie, the class that had become prosperous through the augmentation of industry and wealth, made an instrument of this reaction. Having first asserted itself in England, the individualistic reaction clamorously exploded in France with the Revolution of 1789. But the French Revolution did not signal the definitive victory of individualism against the absolutist State; absolutism still resisted in the XIX century and the battle continued even in this century. The entire first half of the XIX century was filled with this great drama, formed by the struggle between the individual and the State. The affirmation of the individual against the prepotency of collectivity was the most important historical fact of the XVIII and XIX centuries.

Individualism permeated, in this way, all the thought of the XIX century, and it asserted itself in every field. In the field of economics, it is called *free trade* or *laissez-faire*, in the political field *liberalism*.

Liberalism, therefore, is nothing more than the demands of the individual against the excesses of organized collectivity, that is, of the State.

The individualist demands, having spread to other countries, penetrated very rapidly into Italy as well, where they found, however, entirely particular conditions. In other countries of Europe, the individualist assertion had been preceded by three centuries of *national* assertion: indeed, the excesses of absolutism were due precisely to the necessity for the formation of the great European States, which represented the political organization of the great dominant races in Europe. In Italy this affirmation had not arrived. As such, Italy found itself in the XIX century needing to resolve the liberal problem, when it had not yet resolved the *national* problem, that is, the problem of the political organization of the nation.

The struggle between collectivity and the individual, that is, between the excesses of the State and individual demands, ended, throughout Europe, at least throughout central and western Europe, with the full victory of individualism in the political field, that is, with the complete victory of *liberalism*. And even in Italy the victory of liberalism was full and unconditional. The resistance of the absolutist State, allied with the Church, was long and tenacious, but it has long since ceased. Today, you could not find anyone to be an absolutist in Italy for any weight of gold, and the Church itself has accepted the liberal institutions and allows Catholics to vote in order to safeguard its interests.

We have said that in Italy liberalism still found the national problem unsolved. So it set about to resolve it, as the necessary precondition for its victory. In Italy, we now have this new phenomenon: national affirmation understood as a means for the realization of the liberal idea.

From this phenomenon was born the *Italian liberal party*. Which considered liberalism its essential and ultimate end, that is, the affirmation of individualism in the political field, but it held that that end could not be attained in Italy without the constitution of a national State, and consequently it assumed national independence to be a *means* necessary to reach the liberal *end*.

The Italian liberal party, inasmuch as it was fully conscious that the realization of liberalism required the constitution of the national State, was moderate liberal: thus did it have the great merit of understanding the importance of the national problem for the solution of the liberal problem, and the necessity to contain and moderate liberalism, because an excessive affirmation of individualism would have ended with the disintegration of national fabric and would have compromised the solution of the problem of national independence, and liberalism itself with it.

Independence obtained, and the liberal problem contemporaneously resolved, the moderate liberal party had exhausted its mission. It wanted freedom as an *end*; independence as a *means*. Independence obtained, liberty assured, there was nothing more for it to do. It was, still, well-deserving of the country, for having restored its finances, but, having lost every ounce of political substance, it survived in name only, not in reality. It deviated, degenerated into groups and cliques, without ideas, without ideals, without a specific program; it failed to understand, independence obtained, liberty assured, that there still remained something to do, and this something was the nation's prosperity, power, greatness. Having lost every practical and ideal substance, it wandered indecisively to the right, indecisively to the left, committed many errors and many mistakes, and it bore the greatest responsibility for that sad period of Italian history lasting from 1896 to 1900; in power with Crispi, it prevented Crispi from preparing for victory in the African war, skimping on men and means; in power with Rudini after Adwa, it resigned itself to defeat, bought peace at an exorbitant price from the victorious barbarous king, gave Kassala to the English, and humiliated the nation before itself and before the foreigner.

Nor, to this today, has the crisis of the moderate liberal party been resolved. One part of it is still searching for itself, giving a pitiful spectacle of political inconsistency. Another part, is resolutely bent on the class struggle and has asserted itself as the class party, that is, the *bourgeois* party. Faced with the irruption of socialism, which brought political competition into the economic sphere, and declared itself the exclusive representative of the working class, a portion of the moderates believed it was necessary, in order to combat socialism, to adopt the same guiding principle of socialism, and positioned themselves as representative of bourgeoise interests. Thus, there arose, within the liberal party, the bourgeois conservative movement which aimed, at first, during the Pelloux government, to assume a tinge of political conservatism and anti-liberalism, but quickly realized that it was an error, and above all, that it was not necessary for the realization of its program. Thus, the current liberal-conservative movement emerged: conservative, or rather, bourgeois in the social sphere; but still liberal in the political one.

But it is easy to understand the unfortunateness of this new attitude on the part of the moderate liberal party. To establish itself as representative of a social class which, for the economic function that it exercises, appears necessarily privileged, as the *bourgeoisie* is, is a huge political error. A party of the bourgeois class is, by definition, antipathetic, or rather, hateful, to the masses. And I add that a party of this sort must be fought, in the name of national interest, just as the Socialist party must be fought. *Class politics, no matter what class is favored, whether it be the bourgeois class or the proletariat class, is necessarily antinational.* **National politics are the only politics suitable for the nation.**

In conclusion:

Nationalists are not moderate liberals because today's moderate liberals, having no more freedom to conquer, nor political independence to secure, for the nation, have exhausted their program.

Moreover:

Nationalists, for even greater reasons, are not conservative liberals, because today's conservative liberals are representatives of the bourgeois class and nationalists, who represent the interests of the entire nation, are not, therefore, a class party.

This is how things now stand. As for the future, will today's moderate liberals want to give an essentially national content to their program? Let us hope so, indeed, let us help them to move in this direction. But when that happens, moderate liberals will no longer be moderate liberals, **they will be national liberals**, or rather, **nationalists**.

Why Nationalists Are Not Democrats, Nor Radicals, Nor Republicans

The individualist idea is, by its very nature, expansive and exclusive. It is natural, therefore, that liberalism not be limited to demanding the *freedom* of the individual, that is, that it not be merely *liberalism*, but that it affirm the predominance of the individual, and be, therefore, *democracy* as well. *Democracy is nothing but the extreme manifestation of individualism in the political field.* Liberalism, to safeguard the freedom of the individual before the State, wanted the mass of individuals to have *control* over the government of the State; democracy asserted the necessity of giving the *government* itself of the State to the mass of individuals making up the people. Hence, the concept of *popular sovereignty* that is particular to democracy. Democracy no longer conceives of the State as representative of the nation, perpetual entity that is *immanent throughout the centuries*, but as representative of the *people*, that is, of the individuals *presently existing*.

While democracy considers individualism from the point of view of the surest *means* to realize it, that is, participation of people in the government, *radicalism* considers individualism in and of itself. Originating in England, radicalism is nothing more than *integral individualism;* it wants, that is, the fullest affirmation of the individual in all areas.

And it is natural, then, that extreme individualism should be, as regards the form of government, essentially *republican*. The republic seems, in fact, the most suitable form for realizing democracy, insofar as every residue of the representation of national interests as a perpetual entity has been eliminated, and the election of a Head of State ensures that even he is representative of the interests of the people, or rather, of the individuals *presently existing*. But be aware, however, that when extreme individuals speak of a republic, they always mean a *democratic republic*, for the republic is in itself merely a form that can assume any content. And the republic can, like the monarchy, assume such a content as to ensure the perpetual interests of the nation: notable examples include the Venetian Republic, and the ancient Roman

Republic.

But individualism did not stop there. It wants to operate not only in the *domestic* sphere, but also in the *international* one.

And in the international camp, extreme individualism becomes *humanitarianism, pacificism, internationalism. All these are forms in which individualist egoism asserts its absolute preeminence [over the interests] of national collectivity.* Indeed, preaching *universal peace, the solidarity of all men*, one tends to suppress the collectivities presently existing, which are the nations (for to suppress the organization of a society signifies suppressing the society [itself]) by recognizing a single collectivity, *the society of all men.* **But a society of all men does not exist.** Society is another word for a complex of men having common interests to be satisfied, and an organization to satisfy them with. Now, common interests are determined when the union of forces is necessary to face and conquer other, adverse forces, or, in other words, a human society does not form and does not organize except to protect its interests against the conflicting interests of other human societies. This is why we said at the beginning that *a society of all men will not exist until humanity is put into conflict with the inhabitants of the Moon or those of Mars!*

Therefore, this is evident: that individualism, preaching the solidarity of all men, **in essence teaches the lack of any social solidarity and therefore uniquely affirms individual egoism**. When the society of humanity is destroyed, all that remains are individuals!

What has been delineated thus far, then, is the pure conception of extreme individualism. Lately, especially in Italy, another element has intervened to modify this conception: socialism, which has brought the affirmation of extreme individualism from the political sphere to the economic one. Hence a crisis, from which extreme political individualism has not yet exited: and which has led and will moreover lead to the orientation of extreme political individualism toward extreme economic individualism, or rather, toward socialism. Indeed, democracy, in Italy, is becoming social democracy more and more. Already, in Italy, one hardly speaks anymore about a republic, but only about a social republic, that is, a socialist one. And even radicalism, inevitably, must, in its vital organs, evolve in a socialist sense, and will give rise to the formation of a social radicalism.

It is worth noting that extreme individualism has, by this time, among Western nations, and even in Italy, **definitively triumphed on the domestic front**. There is nothing, or almost nothing, left to accomplish in *the sense of political democracy*. Universal suffrage was the last clamorous Italian affirmation of political individualism. The very peaceful and easy way in which universal suffrage was obtained demonstrates that in Italy today *democracy no longer has any opposition in the political sphere*. **Democracy's domestic program is exhausted**.

The international program is, however, not exhausted, where nations still defend their existence against individualistic disintegration, by fighting tooth and nail under a form of pacifism and internationalism. And by defending themselves, nations defend their society, because the dissolution of societies into individuals would signify the return of humanity to barbarism.

At this point, one understands how nationalism, which defends the supreme interests of the nation as an immanent and perpetual entity, must be unequivocally *against extreme individualism*: consequently, against *democracy*, against *radicalism*, against the *democratic republic*. Not that nationalism today, it should be emphasized, wants to destroy the conquests already obtained by democracy: on the contrary, it thinks that beside much harm, they may also produce some good, especially by the *formation of a genuine political consciousness in the masses*. For these reasons, nationalism *accepts today's democratic institutions*.

But to accept democratic institutions does not mean to be democratic. Nationalism considers democratic achievements as a *fait accompli*, which it has no intention to debate. But *nationalism's ends* cannot include democracy. On the contrary, nationalism clearly includes in its program *the defense of the nation against further exaggerations of individualism, which are the natural consequences of the democratic principle*, and thus the defense of the nation against pacifism, against humanitarianism, against internationalism.

In other words, nationalism wants to save Italian society from individualistic disintegration. Nationalism affirms that races in which the interests of the species are sacrificed to those of the individual are destined to be overwhelmed and perish. And it does not wish that the Italian race perish.

That is why nationalists are not democrats, nor radicals, nor republicans.

Why Nationalists Are Not Clericalists

We say clericalists to designate those who are commonly called *Catholics in a political sense*, because almost all Italians are *Catholics in a religious sense*.

Catholics, or *clericalists*, starting from the premise that the ultimate end of the individual is that of meriting happiness in the other life, set the *religious ideal* as absolutely preeminent, for which man must, on this earth, aim above all to be good and pious in order to merit God's love and Divine mercy. The absolute preeminence of the religious ideal leads, in the political sphere, to a demand that the State be an instrument of the moral and religious perfection of the individual. And since the Church is the specific organization whose essential purpose is to obtain this improvement, the State must be an instrument of the Church, or at least be a collaborator of the Church in this its task.

This is the essence of the clericalist conception of the State. In Italy, the religious question presents itself in a somewhat more complicated way because Italy is the seat of the universal Catholic Church, which, until 1870, also held *temporal* dominion. For the indispensable needs of [Italy's] national formation, that dominion was destroyed: whence a disagreement between the Catholic Church and the Italian national State, which has lasted to this day, with no end in sight.

Until only recently, the Church claimed its temporal dominion, and the restoration of the Pope's temporal power was the cornerstone of the Italian clericalists' program. It is easy to understand how this demand made it impossible for the nationalists, who put the nation's interests first, to have any point of contact with the clericalists, who put religion and therefore the Church's interests first.

Today things have changed substantially. **Today the Catholic Church no longer claims temporal power.** This renunciation (which, thus far, has not been, and it is difficult to say whether it ever will be, an explicit renunciation[1]) is the result of many factors: the most important is the participation of Catholics in political life, which means their acceptance of the institutions in place and of the current state of law; but there are also other significant factors: the Papacy's renunciation of foreign intrigues to the detriment of Italy, as it had done, on the contrary, especially with France, before 1903; the recent declarations of authorized Catholics, such as the Archbishop of Udine, Msgr. Rossi, and the Count Della Torre.

Today, therefore, points of contact between nationalists and Catholics can exist. First of all, the nationalists desire national concord and discipline do-

---

[1]explicit renunciation: The Lateran Treaty in 1929 put this question to rest.

mestically, so that the Italian nation might wage, united and close, its national struggle in the world. Now
that the Church has accepted its unity with the Roman
capital as a *fait accompli*, and that, as a result, a serious reason for disagreement is about to end – they do
not want to reignite and perpetuate, with its inoppor-
tune aftereffects and complaints, a disagreement that
no longer happens to have any reason for being.

   Another important point of contact between
Catholics and nationalists is this: that nationalists –
who prize national interests above everything else,
unlike democrats who in their mania to defend the individual against any restraint of social organization
are by nature antireligious – fully *recognize the high
moral and national value of religion*. Nationalists believe, as a result, that the State *cannot fail to take interest in that highly important and fundamental social phenomenon that is religion*. And since the religion of the overwhelming majority of Italians is the
Catholic religion, the Italian State cannot ignore the
Catholic Church or the Catholic religion. It must, on
the contrary, *take into direct consideration the interests of Italian Catholics, inasmuch as they are com-
patible with the nation's interests.*

   These two points of contact permit the nationalists, under the given circumstances, to be in agree-
ment with the Catholics.

   *But neither of these two points means that
there is a theoretical or a practical coincidence between the two, Catholic and national, conceptions.*

   The nationalists are not clericalists for this

fundamental reason: **they consider the interests of the nation as preeminent and absolute and the interests of religion as accessorial and subordinate**.

Therefore, nationalists do not believe that the State should be the instrument of the Church: they believe, instead, that **the State must assert its sovereignty even in the face of the Church.**

Only, since they recognize that religion and the Catholic Church are extremely important factors in national life, they want – [with] *the sovereignty of the State ever strong* – to safeguard as far as possible, *even* Catholic interests. And at this moment in Italian life, the safeguard must be explained especially with respect to the freedom of conscience of Italian Catholics against the antireligious persecutions of the democratic anticlericalists. In the future it will perhaps be possible to go even further, and one will be able to establish, perhaps, with the Catholic Church, one, if only tacit, understanding whereby the Catholic organization might serve the Italian nation in its expansion in the world.

Why Nationalists Are Not Socialists

What socialism consists in, in its fundamental concept, is clear. Socialism begins with the premise that work is the sole source of value. And from this premise, which is erroneous because economic value does not depend on work, but on the *scarcity of goods* – there are many things of great value that cost almost no labor at all (for example, a diamond) – socialism draws the conclusion that the current economic system is unjust because it does not attribute everything produced to the *worker*, but gives a portion of it to those who did not contribute to its production, that is, to the *capitalist*. The goal of socialism is, therefore, to abolish *the extra profit* of the capitalist and to *attribute the entire result of production to the workers*. The means to obtain this: abolition of private ownership of capital, and the substitution of *collective ownership* for private ownership of capital.

From this it follows that socialism, despite its name, **is nothing but the ultimate expression of individualism**. What occupies and preoccupies socialism is *the material or economic well-being of the individual*. So much so that socialism has its own particular philosophy, *historical materialism*, which assumes the economic well-being of the individual to be the goal of all economic actions, and therefore the cause and the explanation of all social life. The belief being, therefore, that the basis of everything is the economic well-being of the individual, this must be the preeminent and all-encompassing goal. And since the current economic system, if it were even useful to the nation, does not fully correspond to the individual interests of the vast majority of the people currently alive, another one will need to be sought, which, with a better distribution of the useful effect of production, makes the economic well-being of the individual as great as possible.

Socialism, then, is essentially *individualist* in its end; it is the extreme affirmation of *economic in-*

dividualism. The socialization of the means of production is merely the means to reach an entirely individual end. So true is this that many socialists, realizing that advocating for socialization of the means of production in the hands of the State risked strengthening, in a certain aspect, the State, they pronounced themselves in favor of an *antistatal* direction of socialism, which aims at concentrating the means of production, that is, capital, no longer in the State, but in the *syndicates*. Whence, the *syndicalist* movement, which is *antistatal*, and therefore more clearly *individualist*.

Now, it is natural that nationalism should be in opposition to socialism.

And the fundamental reasons for this opposition are two.

First reason: by advocating for individualist egoism in its most brutal form, that which has economic or material well-being as its sole aim, socialism not only denies the moral values that, instead, play such an important part in life (*all the most beautiful things that we do, we do not do them for our material well-being*); but it *tends to completely sacrifice collectivity, nation, race, to the individual*. Thus, socialism denies the nation, denies the fatherland, is internalist and pacifist; it advocates Malthusianism, that is, the voluntary limitation of births, because Malthusianism, by diminishing the population, ought to permit existing individuals to enjoy a broader material well-being. **Now, all this not only means preparation for the decline and destruction of the race, but also, necessarily, for the condemnation to misery**

of the generations to come. Nature, being violent, exacts revenge. The diminution of the population does **not produce economic well-being, it produces misery**: because the lack of laborers, the high price of labor, gives way, in no time, to the desertion of fields, to the return of extensive cultivation, to *latifundismo*, and then, the ultimate act of a great tragedy, to the abandonment of cultivation, to deserts. It is the history of the Rome of decline, in which analogous phenomena are verified to have occurred. *Socialism inevitably prepares for misery and the return to the Middle Ages*.

Second reason: this is a practical reason of immediate comprehension. Even if we acknowledged the fundamental principle of socialism, if we also acknowledged that the tendency should be toward the economic well-being of the individual, **socialism fails at its goal**. In fact, the *practical value of socialism, even if it were realized* (and it is important to say that the realization of socialism is practically impossible) would be *minimal or null*.

In other words, it can be demonstrated that *the realization of socialism, in Italy, would not improve in the least or in any measurable way the conditions of Italian workers and it would considerably worsen the condition of today's small landowners, small businessmen, and small merchants*.

And the demonstration is **based on numbers**.

The *annual* revenue of the Italian population, net of direct taxes, is around 14 billion lire today. How are these 14 billion lire divided? They are divided like this: *to the workers 11 and a half billion, to the capitalists 2 and a half billion*; that is 83 percent to the workers, 17 per cent to the capitalists.

From this one may quickly see that *even by giving to the workers that entire portion, which today goes to the capitalists, the annual revenue of the workers would be increased by a rather small amount: not more than about 22 percent than what it currently is.*

But this is too optimistic a calculation.

Of the two and a half billion that today go to the capitalists, only about 700 million go to *pure capitalists*, that is, to people who do not work and who live solely off their investment income. The other 1800 million go to capitalists *who are also workers*: for the most part, the small agricultural landowners, small merchants, and small businessmen. These worker-capitalists will absolutely have a right to a redistribution for their labor, even in a socialist regime: so it must not be thought that all the 1800 million will be redistributed to pure workers, but only a portion of it. And just as there are many small capitalists in Italy, perhaps not even half of the 1800 million could be redistributed; let's assume that half could be redistributed (and that is a lot): there are 900 million which, together with the 700 of the pure capitalists, come to a total of 1600 million that can be redistributed.

Thus, with the realization of socialism, Italian workers who today have a total annual income of 11 and a half billion, that is, 11,500 million, would see it, in the best of hypotheses, rise to 13,100 million, with an augmentation of about 14 percent.

That means that the *average* income of workers would grow by 14 percent: and thus, that **a worker who today has an income of three lire a day, with the realization of socialism he would have an income of three lire forty-two cents.**

And it is worth noting that all of this presupposes that, with the realization of socialism, the total net income of the Italian nation would *not diminish*, whereas **it is certain that it would diminish**, because, in the absence of the drive of individual interest and competition, in the organization of production, *production would become more expensive.*

In conclusion: 1) *a colossal economic revolution made by a paltry improvement that a few years of economic progress today are enough to bring to the workers, and which would probably be absorbed by [the expenses of] the socialist bureaucracy anyways; 2) a perceptible worsening of the conditions of small landowners, small businessmen, small merchants.*

Magnificent result!

Nationalism clearly sees all this, and since it too wants the economic well-being of the individual, *insofar as it is the consequence of the prosperity of the nation*, it turns to the workers and tells them that only *by means of the affirmation, wealth, and prosperity of the Italian race, can they realize an effective, perceptible, and lasting improvement in their economic conditions.*

Nationalism says that the Italian economic problem is not the problem of *distribution*, but of the *augmentation* of wealth. It is not by distributing our still miserable wealth differently that the Italian workers will augment their well-being: **with a different distribution of Italian income a few rich people might disappear, but everyone else would remain equally poor**. The economic well-being of the Italian workers will only grow with the overall augmentation of Italian income and wealth.

Now, is it possible to augment this wealth? And in what measure?

It is possible and in great measure.

In fact, if we compare the Italian wealth of forty years ago with that of today, we see that it has grown from 40 to 80 billion. And, in fact, the average wage in Italy, over the last forty years, *can be said to have doubled.*

If, however, we compare Italian wealth with the wealth of the more advanced great nations, we will see that the distance still to be covered is immense. France has a wealth of 300 billion, England 350, and Germany 400.

Now if, while continuing in our economic ascension, we could reach, I do not say the wealth of France, but half the wealth of France, we would have already doubled our current wealth. The increase of the wealth of a nation does not only mean the increase of wages and of capital income, it means also the spread of property, penetration of ownership into the lowest social strata. In fact, in France and England, the peasants, the workers, possess bonds and corporate shares.

Thus, increasing our overall wealth, our workers can be assured of seeing *their income doubled* in several lustra. If, in fact, socialism is much further off into the future and we see centuries ahead of ourselves before it is realized, economic progress proceeds every day, and if we know how to be prudent, united, determined to assert ourselves before foreign competition, we can obtain in a relatively short period of time this *doubling* of income.

We ourselves will enjoy it if we are young, our children will enjoy it *for certain*.

Nationalism promises this. Socialism promises this. The choice is up to the Italian workers.

Objections to and Criticisms of Nationalism

Objections to and Criticisms of Nationalism

They are always the same, and they sometimes come from adversaries of bad faith, but sometimes also from indifferent people or adversaries of good faith.

First objection. *Nationalists are madmen who want to drain Italy's finances by redirecting it to armaments and drive it to appalling military adventures.*

Whoever makes this objection knows only a portion of the nationalist program, and conveniently exaggerates and distorts it for polemical purposes. Nationalism, it is true, seeks to *prepare* for war, because it holds that, inevitably, the expansion of the Italian race will lead to armed emigration, that is, to war, and *wants* that this war, or rather these inevitable wars, to succeed. But nationalism does not seek *only* the preparation for war. It also seeks, and this is a very important part of its program, *domestic social consolidation*, through the creation of a national consciousness and a strong national discipline: it also seeks to increase domestic wealth through the intensification of economic production; it seeks the economic and moral elevation of the working classes because this elevation is necessary for social consolidation, for the increase in national wealth, and for the military preparedness of the nation. And, as for the bellicose character, which some wish to attribute to nationalism, it is not true that nationalism desires war at any cost. Nationalism wants to *prepare* the nation for the inevitable future wars: nationalism is simply provident. It is not nationalism that *creates* war. It is nationalism that wants to make it victorious. Pacifism, socialism, do not avoid wars (and history demonstrates this), but *makes them disastrous and prepares for defeat*. That is the difference between nationalism and pacifism. **Pacifism prepares for defeat**: **nationalism prepares for victory**.

Second objection. *Nationalists are clericalists.* This is the everyday refrain. Nationalists are not bothered by it, for well do they know that the accusation is a form of political blackmail, which the so-called democratic parties daily attempt. *The accusation is stupid and ridiculous.* The entire essence, the entire program of nationalism belies it. How can a party *that puts the nation first* be clericalist, when it is well-known that the clericalists put religion first? Only one thing is true: that nationalists *are not anticlericalists*, because they do not put, as the anticlericalists of today do, *their antireligious hatred before other national interests*. In conclusion, nationalists **are neither clericalists nor anticlericalists, they are simply nationalists, they put the interest of the nation before clericalism and anticlericalism.**

Third Objection. *Nationalists do not have a specific program, because all parties desire the well-being of the nation, and, therefore, all are nationalists.* This objection is based on the usual equivocation, between *patriotism* and *nationalism*. Patriotism, which is principally *an attachment to the fatherland, that is, to the land*, is essentially defensive, it is a diffuse and delicate feeling, which modestly stands back and yields to everyone else. It comes out only on great occasions, but in daily life it is relegated to the second and even the third tier. Everything is preferred to it, anticlericalism, democracy, socialism, bourgeois conservation, liberalism. Nationalism, on the other hand, is *attached to the nation, to the race, it is the affirmation of one's own race*. Nationalism, especially in Italy, is therefore essentially progressive and expansive, and it is above all an *exclusive* and *exclusivist* sentiment. Nationalism *places the nation before everything*, it connects every activity to the national interest, subordinates everything to prosperity, to the power of the race. Patriotism is the sauce that is found in every dish, nationalism is itself a good and wholesome dish. The character of a party is not inferred by the secondary and subordinate parts of its program; by that standard even nationalism would be socialist because it too desires the elevation of the proletariat! It is inferred, rather, from the dominant and predominant point of the program and, by that title, **the only national party in Italy is nationalism.**

Fourth Objection. *Italian Nationalism is nothing but a copy of French nationalism.* From whose pulpit, one might say, comes the preaching! Italian democracy is, to be sure, a copy of French democracy, a flawed copy when one considers that democracy arose earlier in France, but only after France had already acquired power and national wealth, and it was understood that, with the fundamental problem resolved, it could turn its attention to other problems, while in Italy democracy came to hamper the work of building national power and wealth! Italian socialism is, to be sure, a copy of French and German socialism, an equally flawed copy because in France and Germany, national wealth having already been already *acquired*, they could think about *distributing it*, whereas in Italy, so poor a country, it was *ridiculous* to think of *distributing* a wealth that had not yet been acquired. These are the effects of international *mimetism*, not Italian nationalism.

Indeed, *one nationalism* does not exist in the same way that, on the contrary, one socialism exists. *Nationalisms* exist. Just as there are diverse nations and races, so are there diverse *affirmations* of various nations and various races. For that reason alone, Italian nationalism is different from French nationalism. In France, a rich country in political decline, due to impressive depopulation, nationalism is the mourning of a past, which by now will not return, in which the nation was poor in economic goods, but rich in people and for that reason it was expansive, progressive, energetic. And since at that time an absolute monarchy, allied with the Church, governed France, French nationalism is absolutist, clericalist, and anti-Semitic. By contrast, in Italy, a poor and prolific country, nationalism *does not mourn the past, it has faith in the future*. And because Italy under an absolute monarchy allied with the Church was oppressed and miserable, Italian nationalism is neither absolutist, nor clericalist, nor anti-Semitic. Moreover, because the principal problem in France is that of reinvigorating the race, French nationalism has a domestic character to it, whereas, given our principal problem is that of wealth and the expansion of the race, our nationalism has an *external* character to it, and it is *imperialism*. Finally, because France is a nation that has attained power, and is poor in people but rich in territory, French nationalism is *conservative* and *defensive*; whereas, Italy is a country poor in territory but rich in people, our nationalism is *expansive* and *aggressive*. As you can see, the similarity between the two nationalisms is only in name.

To Whom Nationalism Appeals

To Whom Nationalism Appeals

Nationalism does not appeal to the weary, to the skeptical, to the disheartened, who are legion in Italy; it does not appeal to the timid, to the torpid, to the fearful, who are multitudinous. Nationalism is protest, revolt, anathema against an age-old incrustation of ideas that have deformed, contorted the Italian soul. Nationalism turns against all the idols of the hearth and public square, against all the current and prevailing ideas contained in vulgar minds: it attacks democracy, demolishes anticlericalism, combats socialism, saps pacifism, humanitarianism, internationalism; it strikes at Freemasonry; it declares the program of liberalism exhausted, because already realized. Nationalism is *revolutionary*, and is unsuitable for the skeptical or timid.

Nationalism does not appeal to the ambitious, nor does it want the ambitious in its ranks. Nationalism says as much, frankly, precisely because it is revolutionary; it does not promise its adepts neither posts, nor crosses, nor medallions. Nationalism is a national religion, it is dedication to oneself, it is daily abnegation. It demands everything and gives nothing. Or rather, it gives something immensely great: the satisfaction of having contributed to the triumph of a great cause, of a great idea, the cause of the greatness of the Italian nation, the idea of the future of the Italian nation in the world. Nationalism asks that we sacrifice ourselves for our children, for our grandchildren, for our great grandchildren, just as our ancestors sacrificed themselves for us. It is in the fulfillment of this great duty, which is incumbent on every generation in the evolution of the race, that the sweetest and most intimate of compensations resides.

Nationalism appeals, instead, to youth, to those who have feeling and faith, and who now turn to face life with their mind free of political preconceptions; it appeals to the shipwrecked of the ideal disaster of all political parties, who have seen, with sorrow, all the other Italian political parties forget the national ideal or subordinate it to all other ideas, all other interests, all other ambitions. To all these, nationalism appeals with faith, certain that they will rush to the battle – compared to which, none was ever more bitter or more beautiful.

Other Books by the Publisher

Fanchette's Pretty Little Foot by Restif de la Bretonne

Je M'Accuse... by Léon Bloy

My Hospitals & My Prisons by Paul Verlaine

Salvation Through the Jews by Léon Bloy

Words of a Demolitions Contractor by Léon Bloy

Cellulely by Paul Verlaine

Ecclesiastical Laurels by Jacques Rochette de la Morlière

Flowers of Bitumen by Émile Goudeau

Songs for Her & Odes in Her Honor by Paul Verlaine

On Huysmans' Tomb by Léon Bloy

Ten Years a Bohemian by Émile Goudeau

The Soul of Napoleon by Léon Bloy

Blood of the Poor by Léon Bloy

Joan of Arc and Germany by Léon Bloy

A Platonic Love by Paul Alexis

The Revealer of the Globe: Christopher Columbus & His Future Beatification (Part One) by Léon Bloy

An Immodest Proposal by Dr. Helmut Schleppend

The Pornographer by Restif de la Bretonne

Style (Theory and History) by Ernest Hello

Fallacies: Part 3, Book 4 of Summa Logicae by William of Ockham

What Is Fascism by Sergio Panunzio

Filippo Corridoni by Alceste de Ambris

www.ingramcontent.com/pod-product-compliance
Lightning Source LLC
Chambersburg PA
CBHW022105020426
42335CB00012B/846